What is symmetry in nature?

Bobbie Kalman

Crabtree Publishing Company

www.crabtreebooks.com

Created by Bobbie Kalman

Dedicated by Crystal Sikkens
For Roberta and Dennis Kemper and their daughter, Kate Rose

**Author and
Editor-in-Chief**
Bobbie Kalman

Editor
Kathy Middleton

Proofreader
Crystal Sikkens

Design
Bobbie Kalman
Katherine Berti

**Production coordinator
and Prepress technician**
Katherine Berti

Photo research
Bobbie Kalman

Illustrations
Katherine Berti: pages 5, 24 (bottom left)

Photographs
Creatas: page 7 (bottom)
iStockphoto: page 9 (top left)
Other photographs by Shutterstock

Library and Archives Canada Cataloguing in Publication

Kalman, Bobbie, 1947-
    What is symmetry in nature? / Bobbie Kalman.

(Looking at nature)
Includes index.
Issued also in an electronic format.
ISBN 978-0-7787-3327-0 (bound).--ISBN 978-0-7787-3347-8 (pbk.)

    1. Symmetry (Biology)--Juvenile literature. I. Title. II. Series:
Kalman, Bobbie, 1947- . Looking at nature.

QH351.K35 2011   j570   C2010-902743-4

Library of Congress Cataloging-in-Publication Data

Kalman, Bobbie.
  What is symmetry in nature? / Bobbie Kalman.
      p. cm. -- (Looking at nature)
  Includes index.
  ISBN 978-0-7787-3347-8 (pbk. : alk. paper) -- ISBN 978-0-7787-3327-0
(reinforced library binding : alk. paper) -- ISBN 978-1-4271-9497-8
(electronic (pdf)
  1. Symmetry (Biology)--Juvenile literature. I. Title. II. Series.

QH351.K344 2011
570--dc22
                                                    2010016400

Crabtree Publishing Company

Printed in the USA/122015/CG20151105

www.crabtreebooks.com   1-800-387-7650

**Published in Canada
Crabtree Publishing**
616 Welland Ave.
St. Catharines, Ontario
L2M 5V6

**Published in the United States
Crabtree Publishing**
PMB 59051
350 Fifth Avenue, 59th Floor
New York, New York 10118

**Published in the United Kingdom
Crabtree Publishing**
Maritime House
Basin Road North, Hove
BN41 1WR

**Published in Australia
Crabtree Publishing**
3 Charles Street
Coburg North
VIC, 3058

Contents

What is symmetry?	4
Line symmetry	6
Is it the same?	8
Insect symmetry	10
Symmetry moves	12
People symmetry	14
Spin it around!	16
Five and six parts	18
Which line is it?	20
Fun with symmetry	22
Words to know and Index	24

What is symmetry?

This building has many shapes. The shapes on the left side of the picture are the same as the shapes on the right. When you draw a line down the middle of the building, you will see that both sides of the building are the same. When two sides of an object match, there is **symmetry**.

This building, called the Taj Mahal, is in India.

You can draw a line down the middle of shapes to show symmetry. When you fold the shapes along that line, one half will fit on top of the other half.

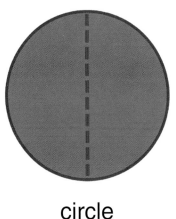

circle

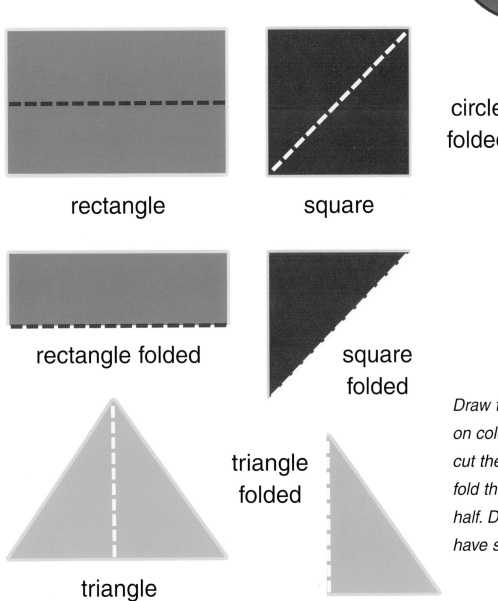

rectangle

square

circle folded

rectangle folded

square folded

triangle folded

triangle

Draw these shapes on colored paper and cut them out. Then fold the shapes in half. Do your shapes have symmetry?

5

Line symmetry

Nature is full of symmetry! This butterfly has symmetry. Its wings look the same on both sides. When the butterfly folds its wings together, the wings fit on top of one another.

line of symmetry

A butterfly has four wings. When it folds its wings, you can see only two wings. The butterfly on the right has folded its wings along a **line of symmetry**.

7

Is it the same?

Some animals have the same parts and **patterns** on both sides of their bodies. A pattern is made up of shapes and colors that repeat. The two wings on the left side of this butterfly's body have the same shapes and patterns as the two wings on its right side. Name three colors and shapes that make up the patterns on this butterfly's wings.

Many plants and animals have symmetry, even though their two sides may not be exactly the same. How are the patterns on these plants or animals not exactly the same?

frog

leaf

crab

apple

claw

claw

Are the spots on both sides of the frog's body the same? Are the lines in the leaf the same on both sides of the center? Are the crab's claws the same size? Are both sides of the apple the same?

9

Insect symmetry

Insects are small animals with six legs. A butterfly is an insect with wings. Like butterflies, many insects fly. Flying insects have wings. Besides wings, what else does this insect have on both sides of its body? Does it have symmetry?

antenna   eyes   antenna

wing   wing

legs

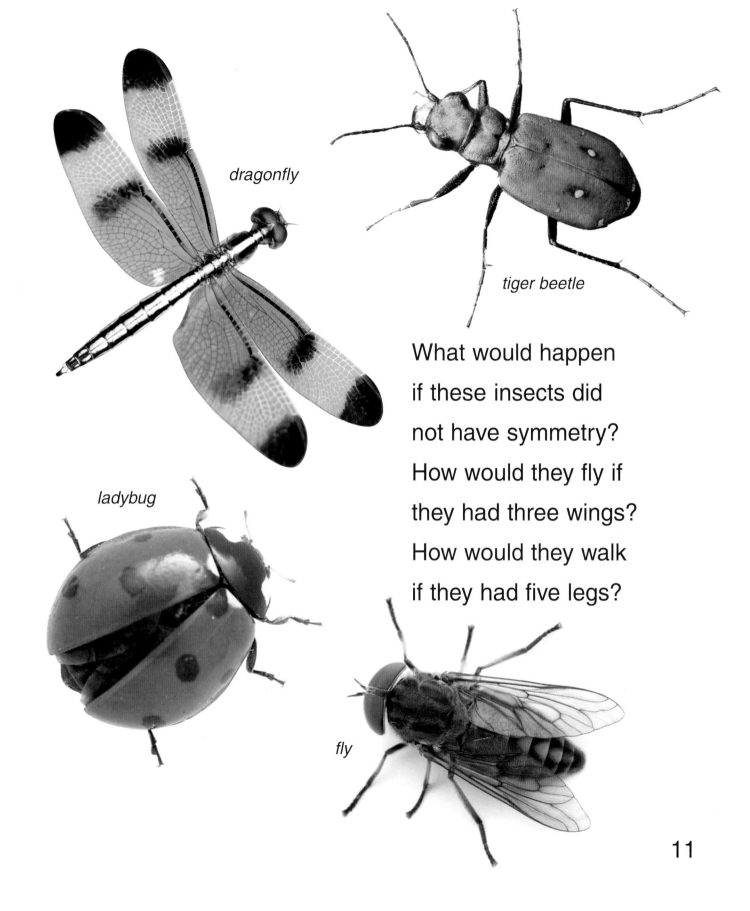

dragonfly

tiger beetle

ladybug

fly

What would happen
if these insects did
not have symmetry?
How would they fly if
they had three wings?
How would they walk
if they had five legs?

11

Symmetry moves

Symmetry helps many animals fly, walk, leap, and run. The animals shown on these two pages have symmetry. How does symmetry help each one move?

Could a fruit bat fly or hang from a tree if it did not have symmetry? How would it fly if it had one wing or three?

A horse has two legs on each side of its body. How does symmetry help a horse run fast without falling over?

Could a tree frog climb a tree if its body did not have symmetry?

fin

Many fish have symmetry, too. This fish has fins on both sides of its body. Its fins help the fish stay balanced and change direction as it swims.

fin

13

People symmetry

Our bodies have symmetry, too. We have two arms and two legs. How many fingers do you have on each hand? How many toes do you have on each foot?

Our faces have symmetry, too. Faces have two sides. Both sides of our faces are almost the same, but not exactly. There are three faces on this page. One is the girl's face as it really looks. The other two faces have been created by making mirror images of only the left side or right side of the girl's face. The made-up faces have perfect symmetry.

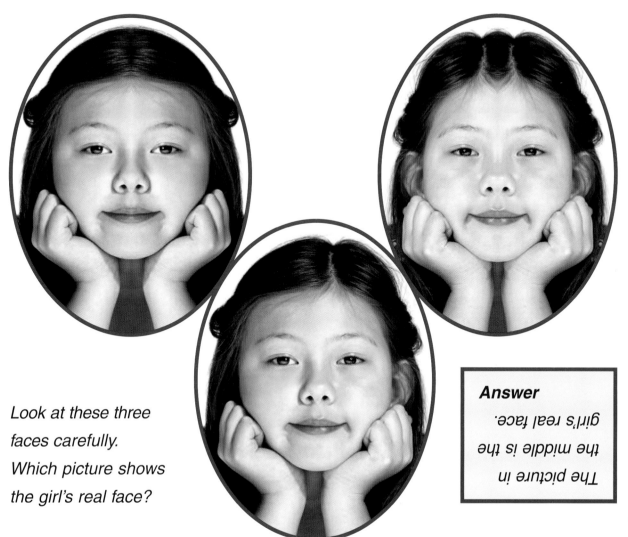

Look at these three faces carefully. Which picture shows the girl's real face?

Answer

The picture in the middle is the girl's real face.

15

Spin it around!

Most of the objects we have seen have **vertical-line symmetry**. A vertical line is an up-and-down line. It is drawn between two halves that are the same. A butterfly has vertical-line symmetry.

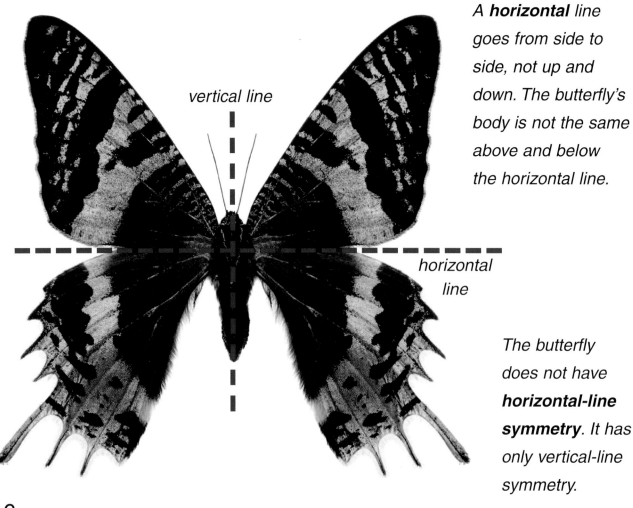

vertical line

horizontal line

*A **horizontal** line goes from side to side, not up and down. The butterfly's body is not the same above and below the horizontal line.*

*The butterfly does not have **horizontal-line symmetry**. It has only vertical-line symmetry.*

Some things have more than one line of symmetry. You can turn them around and draw a line in any direction. The parts opposite each other will be the same. You can spin this flower around, and its parts will still have symmetry.

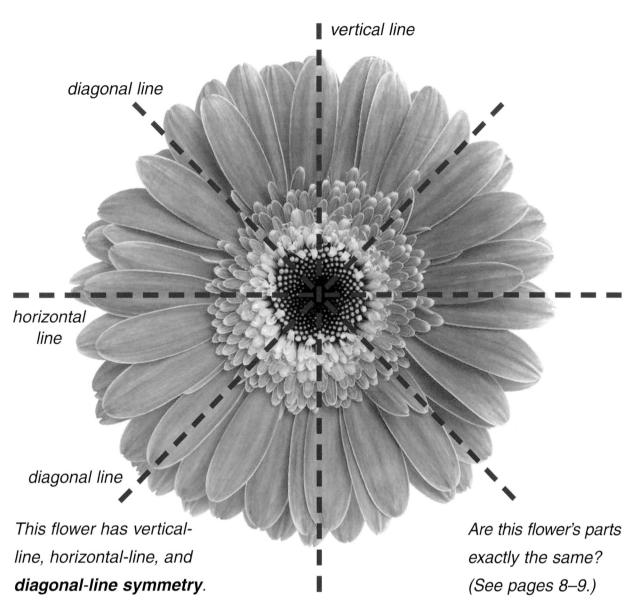

vertical line

diagonal line

horizontal line

diagonal line

This flower has vertical-line, horizontal-line, and **diagonal-line symmetry**.

Are this flower's parts exactly the same? (See pages 8–9.)

17

Five and six parts

Many things in nature have five or more equal parts. You can draw five or more lines of symmetry on them. You can spin them around, too, and the symmetry will not change.

This sea star has five lines of symmetry. It can be folded along the lines of each number, and the folded sides will always be the same.

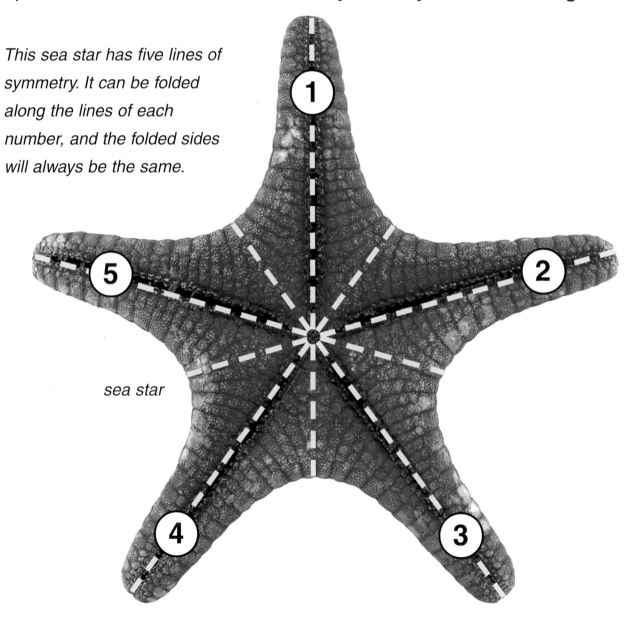

sea star

Sand dollars also have five lines of symmetry.

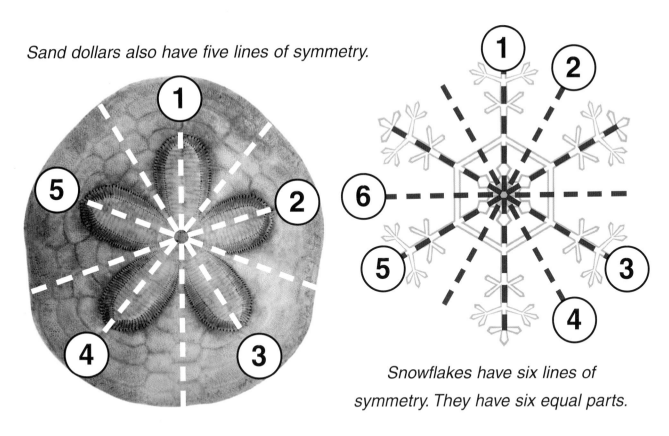

Snowflakes have six lines of symmetry. They have six equal parts.

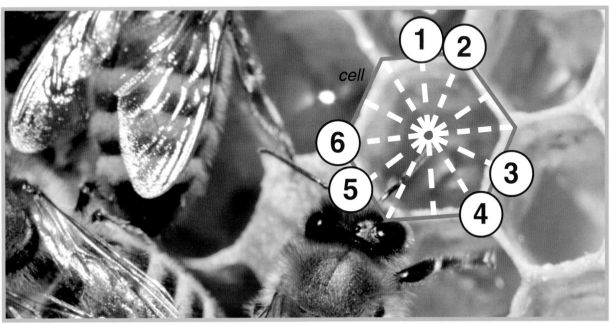

cell

Cells in a beehive have six lines of symmetry, too.

19

Which line is it?

Look at the objects as they are shown on these pages.

Which objects have these kinds of line symmetry?

1. vertical-line symmetry
2. horizontal-line symmetry
3. diagonal-line symmetry
4. five-line symmetry
5. six-line symmetry
6. no symmetry

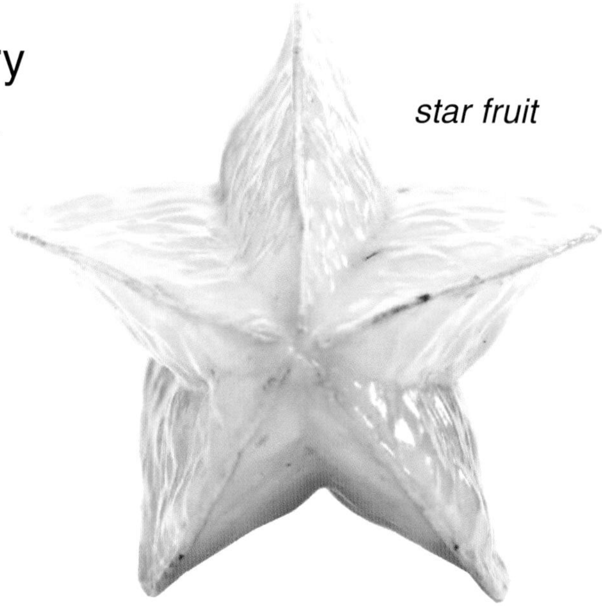

star fruit

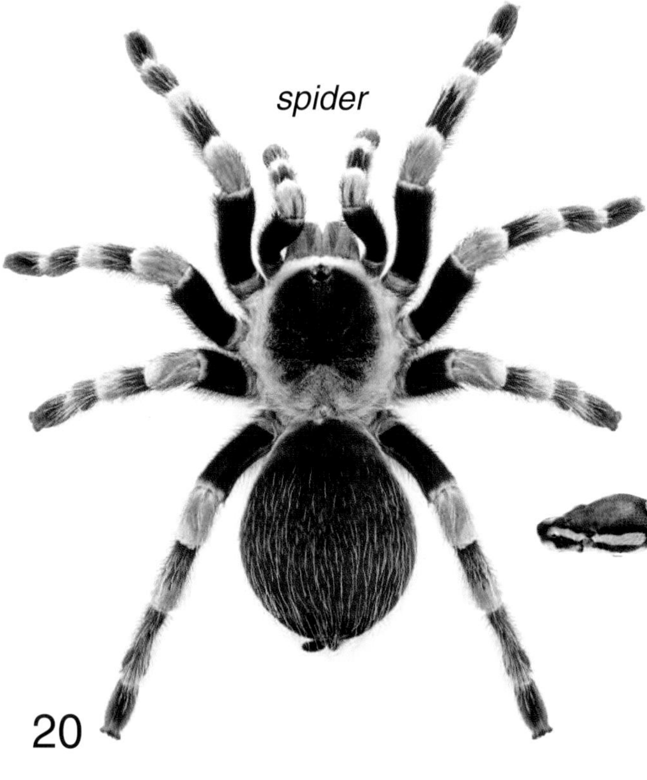

spider

snake

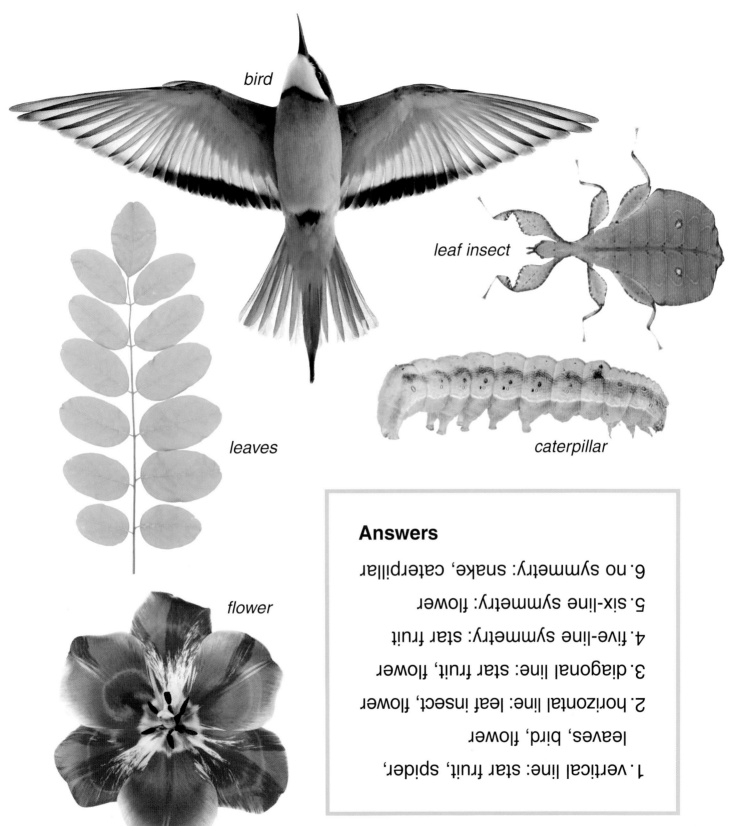

bird

leaf insect

leaves

caterpillar

flower

21

Fun with symmetry

Did you know that when you stretch out your arms and legs, your body forms a five-sided shape called a **pentagon**?

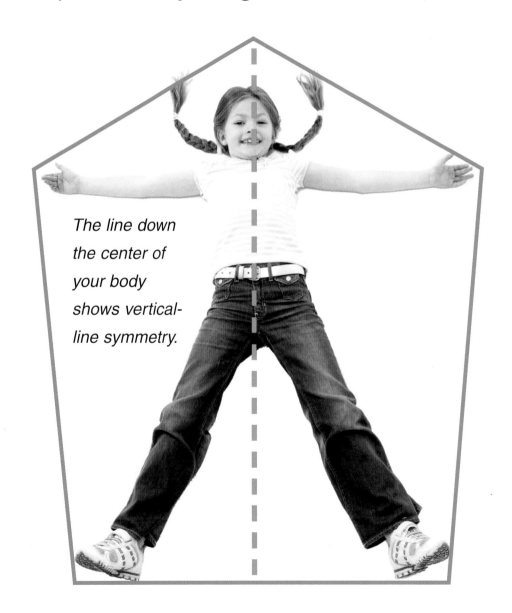

The line down the center of your body shows vertical-line symmetry.

Create symmetry with your face in a mirror.   *Create symmetry using fingers.*

(above) You and a friend can create symmetry by moving your bodies to mirror each other. (left) You can create symmetry in water, too.

Words to know and Index

diagonal-line symmetry
pages 17, 20, 21

five-line symmetry
pages 18, 19, 20, 21

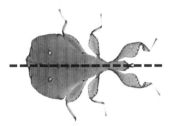

horizontal-line symmetry
pages 16, 17, 20, 21

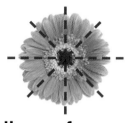

lines of symmetry
pages 6–7, 16, 17, 18, 19, 20, 21

moving
pages 12–13

patterns
pages 8–9

people
pages 14–15

Other index words

animals pages 6, 7, 8, 9, 10, 11, 12–13, 16, 18, 19, 20, 21

butterflies pages 6, 7, 8, 10, 16

equal parts pages 18, 19

faces pages 15, 23

flying pages 10, 11, 12

fun pages 22–23

insects pages 10–11

wings pages 6, 7, 8, 10, 11, 12

shapes
pages 4–5, 8, 22

six-line symmetry
pages 19, 20, 21

vertical-line symmetry
pages 16, 17, 20, 21, 22

24